David Wilkerson says—

This may well be one of the most important books you will ever read. It could turn your life around within the next few hours, in the time it takes to read it.

This book is for those who are seeking true peace of mind and freedom from a life-controlling evil. Even swingers have to face their lonely selves after the music stops. When the bars and discos close, the blues come rolling in. And for millions, Sundays are real downers. Somewhere along the line, the truth about ourselves has to be faced.

At times we are all pitiful actors, wearing false masks and playing phony roles. Yet, somewhere in our innermost being, there is a lingering desire to know and please God.

This book has nothing at all to say to proud, arrogant sinners who refuse to face the truth about their weaknesses. It is written to those who desperately seek victory over self and who honestly admit they need help.

By David Wilkerson

The Cross and the Switchblade
  (*With John and Elizabeth Sherrill*)
Have You Felt Like Giving Up Lately?
Racing Toward Judgment
Sipping Saints
Suicide
The Vision
Victory Over Sin and Self

Victory Over Sin and Self

David Wilkerson

SPIRE ⛪ BOOKS

Fleming H. Revell Company
Old Tappan, New Jersey

Unless otherwise identified, Scripture quotations are based on the King James Version of the Bible.

Scripture quotations identified NIV are from the Holy Bible New International Version, copyright © 1978, New York International Bible Society. Used by permission.

Scripture quotations identified PHILLIPS are from THE NEW TESTAMENT IN MODERN ENGLISH (Revised Edition), translated by J. B. Phillips. © J. B. Phillips 1958, 1960, 1972. Used by permission of Macmillan Publishing Co., Inc.

Scripture quotations identified TLB are taken from The Living Bible, copyright 1971 by Tyndale House Publishers, Wheaton, IL. Used by permission.

Scripture quotations identified TEV are from the *Good News Bible,* New Testament: Copyright © American Bible Society 1966, 1971, 1976.

ISBN: 0-8007-8434-0
A SPIRE BOOK
Published by Fleming H. Revell Company
Originally published by
Garden Valley Publishers under the title
Two of Me
Copyright © 1980 by David Wilkerson
All Rights Reserved
Printed in the United States of America

Contents

Preface		7
1	Two of Me	9
2	Why I Quit Judging Sinners	21
3	Power Over Sin	29
4	The New Plan	43
5	You Have a Right to Be Free	49
6	Free to Choose	53
7	How to End Your Struggle	69

Preface

I started this book in an effort to lead people with life-controlling problems into a life of freedom from sin's power. But I soon discovered it is more than that. It is a personal search for complete victory in my own life. Even though a minister, I hurt just like everybody else. I need power over sin as much as any other sinner on earth.

My search for power over sin took me on a ten-year journey through libraries, commentaries, conferences with Bible scholars, and a thorough study of the Bible—especially Romans. I learned much about the human condition of weakness and the ever-present struggle with evil, but little about the cure.

What I have learned about freedom from sin's power has come out of my own desperation to shake off all bondage to evil.

You will not experience the compelling power of this little book until you read it through entirely. What you read may at first anger you, but don't put it aside until the entire message has been digested. You will discover truth that can set you free.

All I ask is that you read it through, with an open mind.

1
Two of Me

I am a strange creature with two opposing minds in one body. Two distinct life forces in me keep trying to control my actions.

There are things about myself that scare me. Things like a great inner need that can't be explained. Like the constant need for love and fulfillment. Also, those subtle desires that surface on occasion, making me lust for experiences that are contrary to my better nature.

I can't explain why I am such a dual person when it comes to right and wrong. The evil that I hate is always present in me. The good and moral desires are there too, keeping my mind in constant turmoil. It is not an everyday, all-day-long battle, but the evil, at times, tries to overpower me.

Just when I think I've got my act together, things fall apart, and once again I am doing things I really don't want to do.

This war between good and evil is raging in all man
kind. A minister, exposed for adultery, confessed: "M
evil nature held a strange charm over me. It made m
chase false dreams that I knew would fade away. It kep
me chained to a lust that finally destroyed me. It force
me into compromises that weakened me. Its promises o
true love ended up only as a mirage. And, even though
knew I would keep on getting hurt, I followed the dic
tates of my evil mind like an obedient slave."

A former Jesus person, who once played with a reli
gious singing group, tried to explain why he is back wit
the crowd, doing drugs and booze.

"All I know is, there was a terrifying struggle going o
in my body for control. There was an evil presence al
ways in my mind, trying to overthrow every good an
decent thing I tried to do. This evil part of me kep
dragging me down, making me do things I really didn'
want to do. It was such an overpowering presence,
obeyed its every command, and I ended up with feeling
of guilt, loneliness and emptiness.

"Yet, when I escaped all the noises of the crowd an
withdrew from my pleasures, a poor, lonely self dee
within me cried out for satisfaction, like the pitiful ca
of a starving child. The voice cried out, 'Please don'
leave me alone; feed me; help me; give me love.'

"At times a part of me felt angry with God for no
taking the sin out of my heart. I got tired of the battle i
me. The enemy of my soul seemed so strong, and I fel
so weak. The righteous nature in me wanted God to
stomp out all the wickedness, pluck out my overpow
ering, sinful desires, and set me free from my sin.

"I know there is a part of me that wants to obey God. It has nothing to do with churches or preachers or moralizing do-gooders. It is even more than just a desire for forgiveness. It is more than just getting my soul saved. It has nothing to do with the fear of Hell or damnation. It is even more than a need for peace and fulfillment. It is a need, in the very deep of my soul, to know God in a very personal way and to feel His love. Someday I hope to get back to God and be free."

Hundreds of alcoholics and addicts pour out their pitiful stories to me in my office. Almost without exception, I hear the same confession: "I hate it! It's turned me into an animal. It was fun at first, but now it's destroying me. I'm like two people. I'm hooked by a mind habit; now I can't stop myself. Still, deep in my heart, I want to be free. Show me how to get out."

One of my drug addicted teenage friends, in desperation, laid back on his bed, drew out of his veins a full syringe of blood, and splattered on the ceiling the words HELP, GOD!

The homosexual dilemma is one of the most complex of all inner struggles between the dual natures, even though most gays do not think of their sexual preference as a life-controlling problem. To them, homosexuality is normal and they resent any suggestion that they are agonizing over their life-style. Most claim they are not.

From Castro Street in San Francisco to Greenwich Village, New York, I have heard numerous gays tell me how very well adjusted they are. They boast there is no more guilt in them, and that they are proud to be gay.

They tell me over and again that only mixed-up, para
noiac gays want out.

A gay activist leader in San Francisco warned me
"There is not one gay in this city who wants to change
You preachers are simply wasting time. We are no
sick—we are not in need of a so-called cure. We ar
proud, better adjusted than straights—and we hav
every right to resent religious fanatics coming into ou
areas to try and change us. Go back to your wife swap
ping, fornicating straights, and get them to change
Leave us alone."

Nevertheless, the homosexual community cannot ex
plain why a growing number of gays are now admitting
to mind-blowing struggles with their gayness. The heav
drinking, the high rate of suicide, the constant psycho
analysis are clues that suggest the struggle between th
two natures is still raging in the hearts and minds o
gays.

I have a homosexual friend who told me about hi
inner battle with lust and his struggle to be free. He said
"When I started out in homosexuality, a part of me en
joyed it and another part of me hated it. And I hate
myself. A strange feeling began to overtake me, and
started to feel as if there were two of me—two opposit
parts of me, making me frustrated and depressed. I de
veloped an insatiable appetite for sex, and desire pushe
out the guilt at first. I became obsessed with my ow
body. The sad thing is that lust consumed all my
thoughts and energy, and I felt powerless to do anything
about it. I felt my mind tearing in two different direc
tions. One part of me enjoyed wild sex, because it gav

me temporary relief. The other part was sickened by the horrible sex acts that I hated. I was trapped. In spite of all my success, I felt lonely. When the sex drive over-powered me, I turned to alcohol for relief. Somehow I knew that what I was doing upset my whole body system.

"I began to wonder what kind of God would create me with a lust for this kind of sex and make me a pris-oner of my own body. I gave up on any possibility of es-cape. I would just make the best of things as they were. I would find a way to live a dual life and accept the way I was. I'd quit the struggle to change.

"I began to curse God for letting me be born with a monkey on my back. I felt God had abandoned me. Now, another person was controlling me. It spoke to me from far away, from down a deep, dark tunnel. The other me, the good and spiritual me, became just a whimper. Homosexuality completely dominated my personality. It took charge of my life, and I was helpless to resist."

I was listening to a cruising homosexual in the Ten-derloin section of San Francisco describe the terror in his soul. "Friend," he said, "the trading of bodies in a gay bar is the most insensitive thing on earth. It is de-grading and repulsive, because most gay bars are now just information whorehouses, dispensing gossip and pamphlets, and raising money for political causes.

"It is terrifying to have to get your sexual needs met out in the streets. I pick someone up on the street and hope something good will come of it. I keep hoping love will happen. Every Friday and Saturday night, the hope is raised that maybe this time it will happen, my one great love will appear and liberate me from my prison of despair.

"But it never happens. I carry in me a deep sense of fraud, a feeling of being cheated. All the promises I give or receive of lifetime commitments are broken, and what is supposed to be the one great love of my life withers and dies. I'm soon back in the chase, trying to scratch an itch I can't locate. I'm back to loathing myself and feeling abandoned."

Another gay, dressed in full drag and calling himself Reneé, told me how he actually gave permission for a part of himself to emerge and integrate with the other part of himself.

"Reverend," he said, "I can parade around like this because I'm in a gay safety zone. Your terror is caused by trying to control your sex drive properly; mine is caused by trying to score properly. Most gays in my circle are as insecure as me, fearing failure. The coded sexual bargaining keeps you looking. You score, then soon you're back, hoping for a better score. Your hunger is never satisfied; you never get enough! But, brother, it sure leaves the scars. Even my gay friends tend to look at me like 'a twinkie in butch drag.' Their laughter is more cruel than straights'.

"One day I decided to act like the outcast I felt I was. I was tired of broken dreams, endless hurts, and constant loneliness. I made my choice—I would free myself. I knew I had a dual identity, that I was really two people, and only one would finally win. I quit the counselors, put aside my pill popping, and decided to make friends with my body and show it off as I pleased. Reneé is the name I've given my dominant self. Through the day, I am a professor in the classroom; at night, I allow Reneé to surface, and I compete in the pursuit of male trophies.

"In my honest moments, I know it's all superficial. I see my friends battered and abandoned, hurt and wounded by all this destructive competition. Some of my best friends have committed suicide. I feel terribly sad when all alone, even when I have no reason to feel that way. Sundays are downers. What a day of shadows and regrets. Sure I'm gay, but say what they will, I still can't rejoice in it. Reneé bores me now. My friends really don't care about me. The cigarettes are getting stale. Being popular and on top has no meaning. The drinks just depress me. I get restless quickly. What I'm doing is sure dead-end. I'm a forty-two-year-old gay in drag, strutting around trying to deny a tragedy."

I know of one homosexual who thought a sex change could end his inner turmoil. He writes: "I couldn't stand to act as a man. I tried to; even got married, but was soon divorced. I decided there was no help for me, so I entered the gay world and gave in to all my desires.

"My desires took over my reasoning. I was like two people at one time. I wanted to be a woman; I thought like a woman; so why couldn't I be a woman? I found a doctor and had an operation that changed my sex. I believed I had gone too far for God to forgive me, so I appeared in a nightclub as an exotic dancer. But my sex change didn't bring peace to my heart. I settled for lust, for the thrill of the moment, the evening out, the expensive clothes, fine foods, jewelry, drinking, and attractive escorts.

"But when I was alone, I still had to face myself. Looking in the mirror, a woman peered back at me, but I was the same person I'd always been on the inside. I still felt lonely, rejected, and my battle continued.

"I found it wasn't easy coming out. There is always guilt and fear of being discovered. But slowly you harden yourself until it stops bothering you so much. You have days when it still bothers you, but you make excuses or get drunk and high to forget. At first your body rebels against unnatural acts, but you force yourself to conform, until it is no longer painful. Then you end up telling yourself these acts are natural and beautiful to you. Days, weeks, and years go by, and excuses keep you from ever facing the truth."

The Struggle to Be Holy

I have read the pitiful confessions of monks who have shut themselves up in monasteries for years, trying to conquer their evil passions. Still, their evil imaginations almost drove them insane. They did not achieve power over lusts through isolation from society. Just when they thought they were freed from lust and that all fleshly desires were under control, they would fall under a spell of runaway passions and unbridled evil thoughts.

One certain monk lived for fifty years in a subterranean cave, trying to bring his body under subjection to the Spirit. Others buried themselves up to their necks in burning sand, hoping to "burn out" their iniquities.

I have read of monks who slept on bundles of thorns and piles of broken glass. Others bound one foot, hopping around on one foot until they lost use of the other. One monk forced his body into a loop of a cartwheel and stayed in that fetal position for ten years, having to be fed by others.

Simon Stylites stayed for thirty years on top of a column, and when too weak to stay there, he had a post erected and chained himself to it. All of these self-torturing methods were inflicted by monks trying to do away with the evil presence in them. They were trying to annihilate that part of them that lusted after sin.

In the Middle Ages, long processions of flagellants traveled from country to country, moaning, weeping, singing sad songs of repentance, and whipping their bare backs as they marched. Thousands joined these processions in an effort to "whip out the evil."

Saint Etheldra believed her flesh was so evil and dirty, she refused to wash it. She walked about, unwashed and covered with filth, revered as a saint because she had supposedly conquered her flesh.

I read the Bible and discover I am not the only person caught in a struggle between good and evil. David was a man loved by God. Yet he committed adultery with Bathsheba, then murdered her husband to keep him from discovering she was pregnant. He was driven to despair. He admitted, "My sins are over my head. . . . They are too high for me. I can't understand myself. . . .

There is no soundness in my flesh. . . . There is no rest in my bones because of my sin. My loins are filled with a loathsome disease" (Psalms 38:3–7).

Paul the apostle said, "My own behaviour baffles me. For I find myself doing what I really loathe but not doing what I really want to do. . . . I often find that I have the will to do good, but not the power . . . when I want to do good, only evil is within my reach. . . . [It] makes me a prisoner to the law of sin which is inherent in my mortal body. For left to myself, I serve the Law of God with my mind, but in my unspiritual nature I serve the law of sin. It is an agonising situation, and who can set me free from the prison of this mortal body? . . . Christ" (Romans 7:14–25 PHILLIPS).

Two of Paul, also? Yes! It was an agonizing battle in him between a spiritual and an unspiritual nature locked in constant struggle. This agonizing wretchedness Paul describes is the most frightening experience a person can possibly endure. It is a dreadful fear of losing control—a dreadful fear of angering God by giving in to secret sin once too often, or worse, being given over to its control.

The victim who gives in to the law of sin begins to think, "What do I have to do to get victory over this evil in me? I've cried a river of tears—I've tried willpower—I've condemned myself—I've made a thousand promises to change—I've read everything I can get my hands on about how to become holy. But I'm at the point of exhaustion. Will God give up on me until I learn how to struggle free? How can I stand up against such a powerful force pulling me down? What's the use?"

Those who don't have this tremendous inner struggle

have either come through it by faith or they are dishonest people. They are not grieved by their sins, because they choose to overlook them. Some have become hardened by their sins, and they no longer feel any pangs of conscience. Others have designed for themselves a framework of elaborate excuses and justification for everything they do, absolving themselves of all weaknesses and faults. It is a common practice of those who discover they have a life-controlling problem to study history, psychology, sociology, and religion—to find justification for their behavior.

But the honest seeker can't beg off so easily and live with himself. He must see his ugly carnal side and admit, "I am sold under sin as a slave. There is nothing good in me without God. I am weak, frail, sin-prone, in need of the Lord's help daily." Actually, the holier a man becomes, the more aware he is of his own sinfulness.

Over one hundred years ago, the great Scottish preacher, Alexander Whyte, called for honesty in admitting to the battle between the two natures in us. He wrote:

Writers have been afraid to speak out the whole truth about their tribulations. The truthful person must admit there has not been another with so weak and evil a heart as mine, no evil life quite like mine; no sinner beset with as many temptations and trials as me. He must admit to his own experience of inner sinfulness; that his sin is malignant; that sin, at times, still has dominion over him; that indescribable evil lurks in his heart; that all this goes on in his own heart. This is the everyday agony of every man among us whose eyes are open to his own heart.

There is nothing else of which you can be so sure and certain as the sin and misery of your own evil heart; your own self-seeking, envy, malice, pride, hatred, revenge, and lust.

2

Why I Quit Judging Sinners

One day I took a long, honest look into my own heart, and I didn't like what I saw. I saw a minister who preached holiness to others, only to wage a private battle with the same evil presence that is in all sinners. I have discovered since that some of these famous ministers, who cry so loudly about the corruption of society and the evil in the land, are fighting their own personal battles against lust. It's possible to be a world-famous evangelist, moralizing about the corruptness of sinners, and be as phoney as the world's worst hypocrite.

> Prepared as you are to instruct others, do you ever teach yourself anything? You preach against stealing . . . but are you sure of your own honesty? You denounce the practice of adultery, but are you sure of your own purity?
>
> Romans 2:21 PHILLIPS

I am at the place that I believe it is the uncharitable Christian, so harsh and unforgiving, who drives the sinner away from the redeeming power of Christ. The church often drives people with life-controlling problems to reckless abandon and despair by their phoney, pious ferocity against their sin. Christians, who are themselves victims of all manner of temptations, often shut out the habituated by telling them they are hopeless cases. This judgmental attitude says to the sinner, "Keep going deeper into your sin! You are hopeless! The Bible condemns you, so give yourself over to your iniquity. You are already lost, so we won't waste our time trying to help you."

A young lesbian who attended one of my meetings told me of her difficulty with church people accepting her—even after her conversion to Christ.

"I wish Christians would quit 'totem poling' sins and treat everybody alike. They tend to put homosexuals on the bottom when it comes to being concerned about them, and on top of the pole when it comes to judging them as hopeless.

"I get tired of Christians accepting converted adulterers, prostitutes, alcoholics, masturbators, and then recoiling like vipers when homosexuals seek help. They seem on the verge of throwing up when they talk to me; they watch my every move; they eyeball and analyze me, looking for errors. They can't forget my past, as if Jesus came into this world to save everybody but homosexuals."

No wonder sin is driven underground. No wonder

people with life-controlling habits tend to react violently. These troubled souls are degraded; scorn is heaped upon them by a church that wants nothing to do with "queers," "faggots," and "nellies." We have all become very adept at heaping scorn on those we consider hopeless sinners. The scorn and smirk of Christians is one of the greatest causes of injury to those who indulge in sensuality.

We stigmatize people with life-controlling problems. We take away their character by thinking of them as hopelessly hooked. We are so offended by their practices, we have made their sins so scandalous, we turn them into outcasts with no hope of return. We help to destroy their hunger for God by bringing down on them an avalanche of reproach and unforgiving wrath.

If you rob a sinner of his character, if you take away his dignity, if you focus only on his failures, if you treat him as a nonperson, if you shut off all his roads of retreat—he is driven to hardness. He becomes calloused and begins to fight back because that is all that is left for him. It is an easy step from hardness to violence. Humiliate the sinner, take away his sense of worth, and soon you will have driven him to total remorse. If there is no God in him to support him, he will lose all hope and finally give himself over to those who will accept him. Then he often uses that hostility as an excuse to remain in his sin.

My compassion for hardened sinners has been sorely tried. I've seen gangs of leather-clad sadomasochists parading down Folsom Street in San Francisco, flaunting their perversion. They carry nail-studded belts, heavy chains, whips, and other such sadomasochist paraphernalia.

Drag queens strut around, proud, thumbing their noses at straight society. I have had countless numbers of gays call me a fanatic and a fraud. They have cursed my honest efforts to help them—they have thrown my books into the gutter, jumping on them, reviling the author with torrents of cursing.

It is then that horrible thoughts begin to surface in me. I think to myself, "God, they are hopeless. They don't want You; they don't want help. I'm wasting time. Maybe an earthquake is the only language they can understand. Why preach cure to proud people who won't even admit they need help?"

But when I go down to the Tenderloin in San Francisco and talk to those who have hit rock bottom—stoned, bombed out, at the end of their hope—something beautiful happens. Sinners tend to get honest when desperate. The truth surfaces when the games are all over. The phoney fronts, the make-believe facades, all come tumbling down. And suddenly you find just another poor, lost sinner needing the love and compassion of Christ. They weep out pitiful confessions of being kicked around, abused, used, rejected, and misunderstood.

I cannot explain the joy of seeing broken bodies and minds restored by the power of God. That is what draws some of us back time and again to the streets, willing to suffer abuse from the hardened Christ-rejectors. It may be only one out of a thousand who admits to a need or who hurts enough to want to change. But God will lead us to that one—and no power on earth or in Hell can hinder the Holy Spirit from zeroing in on that hungry heart to bring healing.

Paul the apostle said, "God has shown me that I should call no man unfit or unclean" (Acts 10:28).

Searching for a Solution

For years I have been trying to find the key to power over sin. I see in me so many hurtful things, and I yearn to be free from the bondage of my flesh.

My search for power over sin took me on a ten-year journey through libraries, commentaries, conferences with Bible scholars, and a thorough study of the Bible—especially Romans. Everything I read and heard clearly described the human condition of weakness and the ever-present struggle with evil. From Paul the apostle to church leaders such as Origen, Cyprian, Chrysostom—from Augustine to Luther, Calvin, Zwingli, Wesley, and even modern theologians and scholars—all of them described the battle, and all of them admitted they, too, were in the same struggle. In one way, it was reassuring to me that I was not some kind of freak Christian and that the shame for the sin in my own heart was shared by the godliest men who ever lived on this earth. But in another way, it was discouraging to learn so much about the struggle and so little about the cure. Like Paul, they all asked the one great question: "Who will deliver me from this wretchedness in me? How can I be set free from my sinful nature?" And, like Paul, they all answered, "Through Jesus Christ the Lord."

Fine! Christ is the cure. Paul knew that; the church fathers knew it; and I know it. But just what does that mean? That's like saying: Light is caused by the sun. How is Christ the cure? How do I get His great power into my puny body? How do I plug into that supernatural source of righteousness? It is not enough to tell me Jesus can save me and keep me from all sin. It is not enough to say—Simply believe and be cured. It is not enough to say—Freedom comes by faith.

Paul tried to explain the steps to power over sin in his letter to the Romans. He talks about the struggle between an old man and a new man. He warns Christians against being carnally minded and that victory over sin is contingent upon being spiritually minded.

Two men in me? Two laws at work in me? Two minds seeking control of me? Two spirits in combat? Frankly it is all confusing. I read many scholarly interpretations of what Paul is supposedly saying, and I was left even more confused. Scholars disagree on the true meaning of Paul's message in Romans. Even Peter had difficulty understanding certain of Paul's arguments. "As also in all his epistles, speaking in them of these things; in which are some things hard to be understood" (2 Peter 3:16).

I can't believe the path to power over sin is a dark deep secret that would take years to comprehend. You see, I need help right now. The clues can't wait. If I don't understand how God works and what He expects me to do, I will be down and out. Sin could overpower and destroy me, unless God throws me a lifeline of truth.

What is really needed is for God to come down to my earthbound, confused, sin-prone soul and show me how to break sin's spell.

3
Power Over Sin

I thought that the way to get power over sin would be to study the origin of sin. In other words, where did sin come from and how did I get infected with it? But what a long, involved study that is. It's a rather complicated story of a star war that took place before I was born, when the chief angel, Lucifer, led an army of one-third of God's angels in an insurrection.

The origin of sin also has to do with man's being born with a free will, including an alternative to commit evil. It has to do with Satan bringing that alternative to the attention of Eve, the first lady of creation. It has to do with both Adam and Eve having their eyes opened to the inner struggle they had introduced into their bodies and minds. How sin was communicated from Adam to the rest of the human race is another one of those theological problems still being argued.

I decided against trying to locate the origin of Adam's sin. I am more concerned about my own struggle. A person afflicted with cancer isn't concerned about entering into a study on how cancer originated. He simply wants a cure for his own disease. It's true the physician should understand the cause of disease in order to find a cure. But the afflicted body is more concerned about immediate help.

I simply asked the Holy Spirit to show me how to honestly deal with the evil that is right now present in me. To me it doesn't matter where it came from, how it originated, or how it got into my mind—all I know is that it is there, that I don't want it to dominate me, and that I need help to overcome it. I asked God to show me the answer in simple terms I could understand. With childlike faith, I have stumbled upon three absolutes that have opened my mind to a new life of freedom from sin's dominion. They are the keys to my victory over the deception of sin. If you, too, are seeking true freedom, study these absolutes carefully.

Absolute 1: We are all sinners. The Bible says, "All men alike are sinners, whether Jews or Gentiles" (Romans 3:9 TLB).

Are some people better than others? Are straights better than homosexuals? Are teetotallers better than drinkers? Are faithful husbands and wives better than their adulterous neighbors?

The Bible sets the record straight, once and for all. *No one is innocent.* We have all sinned.

"No one is good—no one in all the world is innocent." No one has ever really followed God's paths, or even truly

wanted to. Every one has turned away; all have gone
wrong. No one anywhere has kept on doing what is right;
not one.

Romans 3:10–12 TLB

The Bible doesn't waste words in describing what is in
the heart of sinful man. It's an ugly picture we are all too
familiar with. What is in man's heart comes out his
mouth.

Their talk is foul and filthy like the stench from an open
grave. Their tongues are loaded with lies. Everything they
say has in it the sting and poison of deadly snakes. Their
mouths are full of cursing and bitterness. They are quick
to kill, hating anyone who disagrees with them. Wherever
they go they leave misery and trouble behind them, and
they have never known what it is to feel secure or enjoy
God's blessing. They care nothing about God nor what he
thinks of them.

Romans 3:13–18 TLB

It is very important how I view my sin. The Bible says
I am a liar if I boast there is no sin in me. The only way I
can reach God is to first reach deep into my own heart
and drag out all the filthy, evil things hidden there, and
let His light expose it all.

The Bible says, "From the sole of the foot even unto
the head there is no soundness [about us]" (Isaiah 1:6).
Sin is a disease that pollutes every part of our bodies and
minds.

The Bible says my heart is "deceitful above all things,
and desperately wicked" (Jeremiah 17:9). Why is it,

then, that we don't regard our sin as evil and dangerous, and why do we make excuses for it?

We go about cheating ourselves into the belief that sin is not quite as sinful as God says it is and that we are not as bad as we really are. We invent a long stream of smooth words and fuzzy phrases, coined to explain away the corruption of sin.

Sin rarely presents itself to us in its true colors; it doesn't come right out and say, "I'm your deadly enemy; I'm about to deceive you, destroy you, and send you to Hell." Instead, sin comes to us as an angelic apparition, with a kiss, an outstretched arm, and flattering words. Sin rarely seems sin in its beginnings. But even if you cloak sin with smooth names, you can't change its character.

The broad and liberal theology being pushed today is a modern plague that can't even comfort those who preach it. We have too many false prophets in the pulpit who are clever deceivers. They try to absolve sin by painting it all over with a gray brush. To them, nobody is right and nobody is wrong. Everybody is going to be saved; God loves everybody; sin is just inhospitality or hatred toward your fellowman.

But these same "sin silencers" share with all sinners the same inner gnawing, the same sense of guilt and corruption. They leave the loneliness, emptiness, and despair out of their calculations. They can try to make a sinner comfortable with his sin, but they can't provide him with lasting rest and peace. They can't quiet the deep inner voice that cries, "In spite of it all, you are still guilty."

Sin manifests itself in two ways: first, by appearing insignificant and harmless; and second, by seeming intoxicating, pleasurable, and cozy.

Sin almost always creates a false sense of peace and "rightness." Two lovers, caught up in an illegitimate secret affair, say to themselves, "This can't be sin; it has given me such peace and joy. I feel so complete, beyond anything I've known."

This counterfeit peace causes sinners to imagine they are not sinning. They presume that what they are doing is all right because they feel so satisfied, and they assume they are not hurting anymore. But the satisfaction that sin creates is based on an illusion. It is a false freedom founded on error. And when the illusion fades, there is nothing left but sorrow and despair. That is why sin always leads to depression.

Sin causes pride. And pride aborts all desire for truth and righteousness. The end result is an arrogance that puffs at God and all enemies. The Bible clearly depicts the life-style of a proud sinner.

> The wicked, through the pride of his countenance, will not seek after God: God is not in any of his thoughts . . . as for his enemies, he puffeth at them . . . his mouth is full of cursing and deceit: under his tongue is mischief and vanity. . . . He sitteth in lurking places in town. . . . He hath said in his heart, God hath forgotten: he hideth his face; he will never see it.
>
> Psalms 10:4–11

Sinners often think themselves freest from those sins that they are most enslaved to. They can't reform or convert because they can't be convinced of any wrong doing or guilt.

Some would rather die than give up their sensuality. As one gay put it to me, "I'd rather die and go to Hell then give up my gayness. There could be no Heaven for me without gays. I'd sell my soul rather than change."

Sin reigns so completely, it causes total self-delusion. It causes victims to become unacquainted with themselves so they don't know what they really think, or what they love or hate, or that they are habituated and hooked. Sinners eventually become slighters of Christ who hardly ever again think of salvation or righteousness. They hear so much about Christ and know so little about Him, because sin destroys the understanding of spiritual things. It narrows their freedom of choice down to objects of self-gratification and robs them of their power to serve God.

The mind becomes so distorted by sin, it causes men to fear cancer, yet laugh at Hell. They will seek help for a toothache—yet allow their souls to decay and be lost through neglect. What a pity! What folly!

Only as time goes by does sin reveal its true cancerous nature. A man sins and, because he doesn't drop dead, thinks it is not dangerous. His seared conscience gives him no burn pains, and the burden of sin grows so slowly, the suspect has no idea how high it is heaped.

Sin keeps its control over the sinner by promising more and better freedom down the road.

Sin has its own law of hidden gravitation that causes an automatic downward pull. As it gets lower, it widens in scope. It is always contagious and drags down everyone connected with it.

Sin is most desperate in a sinner when he is hearing the call of God. Sin will resort to any kind of deception to keep from losing control of its victim. Sin becomes subtle when the Gospel is near. It doesn't suggest Run or Mock; rather it chooses to suggest Wait! Don't get in a hurry! *Some other time.* If that doesn't work, sin will pretend the voice of the Spirit, telling the inner man to "yield to God; be changed—in a little while."

Sin can lock its victim in a prison of unbelief and turn him into a violent hater of God. People who are totally possessed by their sins become bitter and hostile enemies to Jesus Christ because He threatens their life-style.

Sin offers service to mankind as a substitute for service to God. The path to dignity and satisfaction is then through helping others in need—fund raising, social involvement in many and various causes. It becomes a substitute religion of good works and charitable deeds. The Bible exposes this religion of good works.

> Salvation is not reward for the good we have done, so none of us can take credit for it. . . . We are saved only by Christ's kindness and by trusting Him. . . .
>
> *see* Ephesians 2:8, 9 TLB

Whether open or secret, all sins must be renounced and confessed—or God cannot help you part with them. The cause of most distress is the maintaining of some secret sin. It blinds the eye of the soul and deadens it so that it can't see its sad condition.

No person can be a true believer until sin becomes his greatest sorrow and burden. Every soul that comes to God must admit to "the exceeding sinfulness" of his evil doings.

Absolute 2: Our sins make us slaves. Jesus made it very plain that any man who commits sin becomes its slave. He said, "Believe me when I tell you that every man who commits sin is a slave" (*see* John 8:34 TLB).

We have the dread power to choose our own master. Paul said, "Don't you realize that you choose your own master? You can choose sin (with death) or else obedience (with acquittal). The one to whom you offer yourself—he will take you and be your master and you will be his slave" (Romans 6:16 TLB).

Degree by degree, secret sin brings its victim to a state of hopeless bondage. Every yielding is the taking on of a new chain. It causes a "fixation" on corruptness. When the mind discovers the body is hooked by a cruel habit, it pretends helplessness. "I was destined to this slavery," the mind argues. "God made me this way. How can He judge me when I am not responsible for this evil magnetic pull in me? I've been this way since childhood."

Not so, according to the truth of God. We enslave ourselves by following our lusts to the point of no return. We are drawn away and enticed by the lusts that are at war in our bodies.

It does not come naturally, because we are all born with a free will to choose either right or wrong.

Paul said, "In the past you voluntarily gave your

bodies to the service of vice and wickedness—for the purpose of evil" (*see* Romans 6:19 TLB).

You may reject this concept of slavery being a learned process of behavior. You may blame your problem on some kind of personality defect, neurosis, or some other stress factor. You can keep telling yourself you are not responsible for your actions—but you can never find deliverance from your sin until you accept your responsibility to deal with it. You must *want* freedom.

If you keep on believing your sin is inherited and you are like a tiny cork carried away by a mighty torrent, you will finally give yourself over to your slavery. Why fight it if you can't beat it? Why seek a cure if there is none? Why talk about a cure when you don't admit you are sick?

This fatalistic approach is a clever lie of Satan to keep slaves in line. There is not one iota of truth to it. There is no sin too difficult for Christ to cure, no bondage too powerful for him to break. You may believe you are hopelessly chained to a habit or to the physical charm of some man or woman, but Christ can melt those chains away like wax.

Twenty-two years ago I went to the slums of New York City to work with drug addicts. The greatest scientific and religious minds of that time were saying that drug addicts could not be cured. The then governor of New York, Nelson Rockefeller, had just completed a two-year, multimillion-dollar research program with not a single positive result. In one medical gathering after another, I heard "experts" say, "There is no known cure for a drug addict. He is psychologically and physiologically hooked. The best we can do is offer methadone as a substitute drug."

I set up business for God in an old, run-down mansion in Brooklyn. Yet, I had that nagging thought deep in me, "Maybe they can't be cured. Maybe there are drug-prone personalities destined to live as slaves to drugs."

Every drug addict who walked through our doors parroted the line of the experts. Over and again they argued, "I'm hopeless. I can't help myself. Once a junkie, always a junkie. I was born to end up with this monkey on my back."

What a lie of the devil that was. God helped us to expose it with a documented 85 percent cure rate, and today thousands of drug addicts and alcoholics have been completely delivered from their slavery. Most do not even have the faintest desire for the very thing that once enslaved them.

I believe the same is true of homosexuality. I hear experts, even in religion, tell me this problem is different. I am told homosexuals are born that way. That it is such a deep psychological behavior pattern, nothing can change its course. Churches and ministers are capitulating, and some now reject the possibility or need of a cure. Yet, hundreds of homosexuals and lesbians are right now finding life-changing power through Jesus Christ. A spiritual hunger is being aroused in the hearts of homosexuals all over the world. I believe it is a result of a sovereign work of the Holy Spirit to once again prove Christ demands cure, not capitulation. As sure as the Holy Spirit has broken the back of drug and alcohol addiction, He will break the myth that homosexuality is incurable.

You can justify any kind of slavery if you buy the deception that God played a trick on you and singled you out as a victim for harassment. How relieving it is to lay the blame on parents, on God, on destiny. And how devastatingly final that deception can become!

Converts are constantly being tempted to fall back into that deception. The battle is lost once the mind is convinced that nothing can be done about the sin problem. When old desires return, the evil presence suggests, "Your deliverance will never be final. Give in to the inevitable. You cannot change. Like a leopard, your spots cannot be removed. Go back; you are wasting time; destiny is against you. It was born in you; it's your nature; quit fighting it. Get out of your closet and live with it."

Victory is possible only when the truth dawns, clear and final: I was not born to be a slave. I can unlearn anything I learned! Slaves can be emancipated! Satan cannot make me blame God for freaking me out! I am not a defective creature! I am not hopelessly hooked. I will learn to be free!

There is no such thing with God as "too far down" or "too deeply involved" or "too late" or "too hard."

Humanly speaking it is impossible, but not with God. Everything is possible with God.

Mark 10:27 PHILLIPS

Absolute 3: A plan was devised for our freedom. The law of the Old Testament brought mankind under guilt and condemnation, because even though it clearly exposed sin, it lacked the power to produce obedience. It was impossible for any human being to fully obey all the laws and commandments of God.

Paul said, "Now do you see it? No one can ever be made right in God's sight by doing what the law commands. For the more we know of God's laws, the clearer it becomes that we aren't obeying them; His laws serve only to make us see that we are sinners [or doing things all wrong] (Romans 3:20 TLB).

Suppose you stumble upon a man deep in some isolated jungle, far from all sources of knowledge. He is sitting on the ground, surrounded by a variety of things which he has no idea how to use. He has a piece of raw meat, a container of water, a small crock of dust, some iron chains, clothes made of skin, and a roaring fire.

He gets thirsty, so he picks up the crock of dust and throws it into his face, making his eyes smart. He gets hungry, so he chews on his clothes. He gets cold, so he sits in the container of water. He feels pain in his chest, so he beats it with the iron chains. When he is tired, he lies down in the fire. He tries forcing the meat into his ears to stop an earache.

What torment that poor man would go through because he had no idea how to use the things at his disposal. He doesn't understand the law of fire, of pain, of hunger, or of thirst. Suppose you approach that man and show him how to cook and eat the meat, how to use the iron chains to pull logs for his fire, how to put the clothes on his back when he is cold, how to drink the water to quench his thirst. From then on, he will know it is wrong to do it the old way.

Did you show him how wrong it is to lie in the fire just so you could bring him under bondage? Did you do it to rob him of his freedom of choice? No! You did it to save him from destroying himself.

In that way, God's laws and His commandments are meant for our own good. They are not meant to cramp our free style or hinder our freedom. They are meant to teach us the proper way to use the things created for us by God. The laws of God are designed to show us that if we misuse the world and the things in it, it can never bring happiness or satisfaction—that we will only add to our pain and continue mishandling those things meant to help us.

Let me show you the weakness of this whole thing and why a new plan had to be devised. You can show that misled man how harmful his way of doing things may be. You can show him how to do it the right way. But you can't force him to do it the right way. He may go right back to chain-whipping his chest, throwing dust into his eyes, and sitting in cold water in an effort to get warm, simply because he is used to doing it that way.

God had to send Christ to die on a cross. Stubborn creatures as we are, we keep on doing things our own way and destroying ourselves. God gave us the Law to show us how stupidly we were conducting our lives and to warn us of the consequences, but we preferred to go on doing things the way we were accustomed to. So the Law failed to make us do what is right. The Law was an illustrated lecture that nobody paid much attention to.

That is why a new plan to save mankind from sin was devised. A new way so simple that even a child could understand it. The new plan consisted of believing, rather than doing.

4

The New Plan

But now God has shown us a different way to heaven—
not by "being good enough" . . . but by a new way.

Romans 3:21, 22 TLB

What a predicament! All God wanted to do was share
His love and make His creation happy and fulfilled, but
now sin was driving him even further away from His
love. If mankind kept on that course, God would eventually have no one wanting His love, and all mankind
would be in hiding from His presence. He couldn't permit that.

Man ended up in a hopeless dilemma. The natural
man, created with a hunger for divine love, could not
understand or perceive that love. So man goes off seeking methods of satisfying that hunger in fleshly ways.

Some believe their hunger originates in their belly.

Food becomes their god. "Whose god is their belly," the Scripture says. They mistake their appetite for God as an appetite for food and become gluttons. When lonely, they eat. When depressed, they eat. When that unknown, deep, inner hunger begins to gnaw, they try to drown it in an avalanche of food. It doesn't work. They are never satisfied.

This hunger drives mankind to alcohol! Recent surveys reveal that an overwhelming majority of the population is now drinking on a regular basis. The further a man strays from God's love, the more he drinks. He can stone away the hunger for a few hours, but it always returns with a greater intensity.

Others feel their appetite is in their loins. They develop an insatiable appetite for sex. They are overcome with an instinct to be held, touched, embraced, deeply loved. They shuttle from one person to another, trying to satisfy that deep, inner longing. Some lust after men; others, after women. Unfortunately for them, the spirit is not attached to the loins. That is why sex cannot produce love. Your loins have about as much chance of producing love as your belly. Even legally married people can't produce love with sex. They can indulge in sex frequently and still not satisfy their real need for love. Love is a spiritual, divine gift of God that is not produced by sex. Two people having sex is equal to two people having lunch. Both are satisfying a human hunger but in no way producing true love. Sex can temporarily satisfy human hunger, but it can't satisfy the hunger of the inner man.

It can be said of this generation: ". . . whose loin is

their god." Rather than worship God and accept His love, they seek to satisfy their hunger by worshipping their own bodies and by making sex their god. But it doesn't take long to discover that sex can't produce happiness, lasting joy, or peace.

Perversion is not an illegal sex act; it is refusing God's love and substituting self love. It is worship of the human body. It is making an idol of the loins. And all man's problems result from refusing to recognize that his real needs are spiritual and not physical.

A Final Solution

Since man was guilty and afraid of God and in hiding from Him, God decided to enter the human race Himself through His Son Jesus. The work of Jesus was very simple: He was sent to bring mankind back to God.

> For God was in Christ, restoring the world to himself, no longer counting men's sins against them but blotting them out. This is the wonderful message he has given us to tell others.
>
> 2 Corinthians 5:19 TLB

Think of it! God was in that Man Jesus, going about desperately trying to restore mankind back to His glorious love. The evidence is overwhelming:

> But God showed his great love for us by sending Christ to die for us while we were still sinners.
>
> Romans 5:8 TLB

God got tired of allowing obstacles to come between Himself and His object of love. He determined that never again would anything ever separate man from His love. Yet, sin was still the one great force separating man from Himself. Every time man sinned, he ran and hid from God. Adam did it; Cain did it; David did it; and we are still doing it. God said: *"Enough!"*

God decided to put all the sins of mankind on His own Son, let Him die like a guilty convict, thereby letting all men go scot-free. It would be somewhat like a federal judge choosing an innocent person to pay for all the crimes of every prisoner in every jail, sentencing him to death, opening the jails, and letting all the prisoners go free. Does it sound ridiculous that one person could pay for the crimes of every lawbreaker? Sure it does! But by an act of love we call *grace,* God did just that.

God decided to free, release, and discharge all the sins of the whole world. Christ was crucified and was resurrected; and God said, "My plan is finished. Man can now come back to My love, because I freely forgive him. I release him of all his guilt; I have nothing at all against him. No longer can sin stand in the way."

Forgiven? Of adultery? Homosexuality? Murder? Rape? Incest? Drug addiction? Alcoholism? Stealing? Gambling? Lust? And all other sins known to mankind? Absolutely yes! Total forgiveness without having to work for it or earn it! It is a gift of God, made possible by the death of Christ, received by faith.

Someone asked Jesus, "What must I do to be saved?" In other words, "What is my part in this plan to help

me? Is there a catch? How can I enjoy this freedom from
sin and guilt?"

Jesus answered with a single word: *"Believe!"*

You've heard that all your life: *Believe and be saved.*
But what does that mean?

To believe is to consent to something you have heard.

Faith is something you do about what you know.

For example, a prison warden calls in a condemned
prisoner and holds up to his view an official-looking letter and says, "I have in my hand your pardon! Do you
believe that?"

The prisoner nods his head and says, "Yes, I believe."

The warden opens the letter and reads the pardon
aloud, then turns to the prisoner and says, "You're a free
man. You may leave any time you please."

The poor deluded prisoner shakes the warden's hand,
says thank you, and heads right back to his cell and his
old buddies!

He heard the good word; he believed every word of it;
he even was polite and said thanks. But if he had faith in
what he heard, he would have walked out of that warden's office without looking back.

Even devils "believe" in God and tremble in His presence. You can't be changed by simply agreeing with the
Word. You can't say, "Sure, I hear You; I understand,"
then go back to your sins without doing something
about what you know to be truth. What you do about
what you know is what God holds you accountable for.

Faith without action is as dead as a body without a soul.
James 2:26 PHILLIPS

5

You Have a Right to Be Free

And you shall know the truth, and the truth shall set you free.

John 8:32

There is no other right belonging to mankind more important than the right to be free from sin's power. License to sin at will is not freedom, rather it leads to a demanding bondage.

The freedom Christ offers is the breaking of every sin chain and the opening of every prison of evil habit. To suggest that any life-controlling sin is acceptable to God is to charge Him with cruel negligence and unconcern. What kind of a loving Father could accept His child being held in chains and used as a slave?

Can a Christian keep on indulging secret passions and

stay in favor with God? My answer to that is: Why would he want to? That is like asking, "Can a man be at his best chained in a prison?" Why would any prisoner prefer to stay locked up when a judge stands at an open gate, pointing him to freedom? It serves no purpose to condemn sex sin only as an abomination, as unnatural, or as a perversion or depravity. Those are only the side effects of the real problem—imprisonment.

The Bible says truth sets men free. Christ died to provide that freedom, and He is not about to permit men to make a mockery of it. I am not at all interested in the age-old arguments of what the sin of Sodom was or in splitting theological hairs about what the Bible does or does not say about homosexuality, alcoholism, drug addiction, or other such life-controlling habits. All I know is that when men accept the truth of Christ, it sets them free—period! And just so men can't explain that Christian freedom as the right to sin at will, God clearly defines what that freedom is.

> The old sinful nature within us is against God. It never did obey God's laws and it never will. That's why those who are still under the control of their old sinful selves, bent on following their old evil desires, can never please God.
>
> Romans 8:7, 8 TLB

A New Love

It is impossible to bring any life-controlling problem to a dead stop and remove it without putting something else in its place. Sin won't yield to exposure; fear can't drive it out; it won't self-destruct. There is no such thing as a simple separation from an old habit.

It takes more than a simple act of resignation. It takes more than just a Sabbath or nighttime emotion of sorrow. It takes more than a theatrical surface repentance. The heart will not consent to be robbed of one affection without another to fill the void. It will not consent to be left desolated of love unless a greater love dispossesses the old.

The heart of man revolts against being left empty; it cannot bear to be left in a state of waste or cheerless emptiness. Nature does abhor a vacuum, so to tear away any affection from the heart and leave it bare is a hopeless undertaking. The human heart must grasp and fasten itself to some great affection. It has to have something to lay hold on, to cling to.

Any person who tries to tear out of his heart some kind of pleasurable sin or affection without putting something in its place is flirting with a disastrous situation.

The last state of that man could be worse than the first, with a legion of demons flocking in to fill the void.

Christ is not some kind of "sin plucker" who goes about taking habits and pleasures away from sinners, leaving them clean, but empty. God doesn't take anything from anybody; He simply offers something far better. God doesn't make voids; He fills them. We have God all wrong. We come begging Him to take things away from us, rather than asking Him to flood our souls with the mighty Niagara of His love and give us something far greater.

The love of God and the love of this world are two affections; not just rivals, but enemies. They cannot dwell together in the same heart. But the love of God is so powerful, so all-consuming, it subordinates all other loves. If other affections won't yield, He chases them away.

When we accept our adoption into God's family by faith in Christ, He brings the heart under the mastery of one great and glorious affection, thereby delivering us from the tyranny of old affections.

You will not be free until you set your mind to possess this affection for things above. Don't allow your unbelief to screen out the vision of God's wonderful love. The best way to cast out your impure affection is to invite in a pure one.

6

Free to Choose

Now we get down to the nitty-gritty, the very heart of this book.

Will believing on Jesus Christ as Lord cause all my evil desires to go away? Will I no longer be tempted? If I repent and surrender my life to Christ by faith, will He change me? Will the passions that have an iron grip on me be broken? How can I have power to resist temptation? Can I really become a new person?

First, let me show you what the Bible says on the subject.

1. Faith in Christ dispossesses the sinful nature.

Now if Christ does live within you, his presence means that your sinful nature is dead, but your spirit becomes alive because of the righteousness he brings with him.

Romans 8:10 PHILLIPS

2. He helps cut the nerve of evil instincts.

> Then my brothers, we owe no duty to our sensual nature,
> or to obey our instincts. If on the other hand you cut the
> nerve of your instinctive actions by obeying the Spirit,
> you will live.
>
> Romans 8:13 PHILLIPS

3. He breaks the tyranny of sin once and for all.

> Your old evil desires were nailed to the cross with him;
> that part of you that loves to sin was crushed and fatally
> wounded, so that your sin-loving body is no longer under
> sin's control, no longer needs to be a slave to sin; for when
> you are deadened to sin you are freed from all its allure
> and its power over you.
>
> Romans 6:6, 7 TLB

Now we come to the big question—the question that
has baffled the minds of God-loving believers from Paul
the apostle to today. It is the question that haunts those
who gave up on the Christian way, because it didn't
seem to break their chains of sin. If Christ makes believers dead to sin, if the nerve of their evil instinct is
severed, if their evil nature is crushed—why do they still
discover old evil desires popping up? Why is there still
an evil presence in their bodies? Why are they still capa-
ble of doing sinful things like all other sinners? Why be a
Christian, if it doesn't break the power of sin?

Believers do discover that old desires return, and they
are forced to say with Paul:

I don't understand myself at all, for I really want to do what is right, but I can't. I do what I don't want to—what I hate. I know perfectly well that what I am doing is wrong. . . .

Romans 7:15, 16 TLB

Now if I am doing what I don't want to, it is plain where the trouble is: sin still has me in its evil grasp.

Romans 7:20 TLB

I love to do God's will so far as my new nature is concerned; but there is something else deep within me, in my lower nature, that is at war with my mind and wins the fight and makes me a slave to the sin that is still within me. In my mind I want to be God's willing servant but instead I find myself still enslaved to sin.

Romans 7:22–25 TLB

Paul wasn't talking about an experience before accepting Christ—because he states, "I love to do God's will." He also speaks of his "new life" that tells him to do right. That is not the testimony of a sinner. Paul, at one time, fought this battle after his conversion, and he opened to us his inner struggle. It has been the personal battle of all honest Christians.

It sounds almost like double-talk. It sounds like Christians are no better off than sinners. It seems like the battle never ends. *Not so!* There is an explanation proving the power of sin is broken. Paul said,

Who will free me from my slavery to this deadly lower nature? Thank God! It has been done by Jesus Christ our Lord. He has set me free.

Romans 7:25 TLB

What discovery did Paul make that could cause him to rejoice and say, "There is now no condemnation hanging over my head" (Romans 8:1 PHILLIPS)? What great discovery stopped him from saying, "I want to do right, but I can't"? How did Paul work his way through this dilemma?

He talks about *a new principle of freedom.* This new principle of freedom through Jesus Christ actually stopped the sin merry-go-round, plucked him off the endless ride, and freed him once and for all from its power.

Simply stated, here is how this freedom principle works. Three great truths are involved.

1. Believers are no longer slaves to sin.

We have no obligation to our sensual nature.

Romans 8:12 PHILLIPS

Abraham Lincoln is said to have "freed the slaves" with the Emancipation Proclamation. This legal document declared slavery dead. All slaves were set free.

When this news first spread throughout southern plantations, many of the slaves would not believe it. They continued slaving for their masters, convinced their promise of freedom was a hoax. Numbers of unscrupulous landowners told their slaves it was a false rumor and kept them under bondage. But, little by little, the truth dawned on them as they saw former slaves walking about, taking advantage of their newfound freedom. One by one, they threw down their loads, turned their backs on slavery, and walked away to begin a new life.

Maybe you haven't heard yet, or maybe it sounds too good to be true, but Christ emancipated all the slaves to sin at Calvary. You can now "walk out" on the devil! You can throw down your load of sin, walk away from Satan's dominion, and enter into a new life of freedom.

Let me show you what the Bible means when it talks about dying to sin. When Lincoln emancipated the slaves, the "issue" of slavery died. Not the slave master—not the slave. The slave could walk away free, saying to himself: *Slavery is a dead issue. The old slave in me is dead. I am a free man.*

When someone receives Christ as Lord, what is it in him that dies? Sin doesn't die. Satan doesn't die. Nor does the evil tendency die. The "issue" or the "controversy" dies. Sin created a controversy in the heart of man about who was in control, and the battle between good and evil was the result. God simply emancipated the mind from sin's control, killing the controversy of slavery to evil.

When the Bible says "we die to sin," it simply means that to us the issue is dead! There is no more argument—the matter is not negotiable—mankind was emancipated at Calvary! The issue as to who is in charge is dead!

Paul used legal terms to describe the Christian's freedom from sin's bondage. The same legal terms are used daily in Congress: The bill is dead. The amendment was killed. The resolution died.

The Bible says, "... he that is dead is free from sin. ... Now if we be dead with Christ, we believe we shall also live with him" (Romans 6:7, 8).

What that means is simply this: Since the matter of your slavery to sin is a dead issue, seeing that Christ has already declared you emancipated, you are now free to live as a new person in Christ. In other words, you have died to slavery, so why go back and pick cotton for the devil?

Now the slave could slip back into the field and pick a few more rows of cotton—perhaps through fear or instinct—but that, in no way, made him a slave again. He was free, but he had to exercise his freedom. The proclamation couldn't force compliance, and neither could the slave master force him to return. It was a matter of the will of the slave.

Christ can't make you do right, and Satan can't make you do wrong. Christ declares we are free by faith, but we must act as a free person.

Eons ago, in Hell's court, Satan decreed a law that, as prince of the world, all living souls were his subjects. God's supreme court killed that law of sin. It died because Satan could not enforce it anymore. God declared it unconstitutional and substituted His own law—the law of the spirit—giving Him all rights to the believer's body.

After years of trying to understand what Paul meant by *dying to sin* or *death of the old nature,* I now see how simple it all is. Sin doesn't die, only the *slavery* to it dies. Its power over me dies. So now I don't have to go around trying to die or struggle to feel dead. Nothing in me dies except the law that held me in sin's control. Sin is still present in me, but I am no longer under its control.

Think of freedom from sin as an annulment. Christ takes the believer to His Father, the Judge, and gets an annulment from sin so that He can take that same believer as a bride to Himself. Christ loved us while we were still living with sin; He died to prove that love; and that gave Him the right to annul sin's claim on us.

This annulment makes us dead to the claims of the old affair, but it doesn't stop the old illicit lover from coming around to harass, seduce, or try to press a new claim. Satan never accepts such an annulment without a fight. He will come calling with threats, with compromises, with alluring offers. But legally, Satan no longer has a claim on any believer. Paul wrote, "... having died to that which once held us, we now serve in newness of the Spirit, and not in the oldness of the Law" (Romans 7:6).

No Christian can now say, "I can't help myself. I can't break from my sin." Paul was finally delivered from this kind of talk, and so must we be! Satan can't make you sin now; but your old slave nature can attempt to reassert itself. If Christ did not break the power of sin, the crucifixion was a hoax.

You will always be a slave until you quit excusing your weaknesses by claiming to be helpless. You are not helpless as a child of God. You are not the devil's patsy anymore, so get busy and discipline your wild, stubborn will. A Christian who says, "I can't" is actually saying, "I won't." Pretending to still be a slave is an alibi Christians use to put off facing the responsibility of their freedom.

> And so we should not be like cringing, fearful slaves, but we should behave like God's very own children, adopted into the bosom of his family . . .
>
> Romans 8:15 TLB

> So Christ has made us free. Now make sure that you stay free and don't get all tied up again in the chains of slavery. . . .
>
> Galatians 5:1 TLB

2. Freedom from sin's slavery must be accepted by faith.

> The whole thing then is a matter of faith on man's part, and generosity on God's.
>
> Romans 3:16 PHILLIPS

I have already stated in this book that faith is something you do about what you know. Knowledge means nothing unless it is acted upon.

The children of Israel received the good word that God had given them Canaan for a homeland. That information would have meant nothing at all to them if they had remained in Egypt as slaves. But the Bible says, "By faith . . . they forsook Egypt . . . by faith they passed over the Red Sea" (Hebrews 11:27–31).

The Israelites did not march to the border of Canaan, fire one volley of arrows, and expect all the enemy armies to drop dead. The land was theirs, but they had to possess it "one dead soldier at a time."

What does that have to do with my getting victory over the grip of sin? Everything! Christ settled the issue of slavery to sin by declaring me emancipated from its dominion, but I have to believe it to the point that I do something about it.

It is not enough to say, "Yes, I believe Christ forgives sin. I believe He is Lord. I know He can break the power of sin in my life." You are mentally consenting to what you heard. But faith is stepping out on that promise of freedom and acting upon it.

How? By breaking off with old friends who drag you down. By convincing yourself that freedom is, in reality, yours. Claim it! God said it, so act on it. Shake off your passiveness and move into your new life of peace and freedom with determination and assurance.

Face the facts. All your other methods to find peace and freedom have failed. You cried a river of tears; you made a thousand promises that you broke; you tried self-control, self-denial, and various self-help programs. After all you tried, you still ended up with unfulfilled longings you could not understand. You found yourself unable to stop sinning. You were, at times, driven into sin through sheer boredom and mental depression.

The problem is, you have not yet gotten to the root of your problem. You may have heard that Christ has emancipated you by dying on a cross, but you will never enjoy that freedom until you give God what He asks of you—and that is a trusting mind. He wants you to believe your prayers are heard and will be answered.

But without faith it is impossible to please him; for he that
cometh to God must believe that he exists, and that he re-
wards those who sincerely seek him."

Hebrews 11:6

Faith is simply taking God at His word and acting
upon it. The true believer is the person who can say,
"God said, therefore I believe it. I'll stake my life, my
future, my eternity on it. If God has decreed that I am a
free person—if He tells me sin no longer has power over
me—if He says my faith in Him makes it all possible—
then I accept—I give up my useless struggle—and I yield
all to him. I do believe!"

3. Believers are supernaturally helped in their hour of
   temptation.

There hath no temptation taken you but such as is common to man: but God is faithful, who will not suffer you
to be tempted above that ye are able; but will with the
temptation also make a way to escape, that ye may be
able to bear it.

1 Corinthians 10:13

This is the most powerful and encouraging promise in
all of the Bible for believers who face temptations. God
makes it very clear that no child of His is left alone to
battle against lust, passion, or any habituating evil. Supernatural help is needed and provided.

Believers all over the world are becoming weak
against temptation, and they are yielding to the flesh in
increasing numbers. It seems as though some Christians
now think of temptation as a kind of incurable disease

that won't let go until it destroys its victim. They cringe in fear when temptation strikes, thinking, "Oh, no—here I go again. It's got me in its grip, and I just know I'm going to give in. I have no willpower; I'm too weak to resist."

That is the defeatist thinking of believers who do not know how to claim their right to assistance. *What is this right promised to all believers? It is the right to supernatural help in temptation.*

Do I mean by this that Christ not only delivers a believer from the power of sin, but also helps keep him from going back to it? That is exactly what the Bible says.

When temptation rolls in like a flood, Christ exercises His lordship and does something supernatural to combat it. He "makes a way to escape," so that believers can survive the ordeal or, in other words, "bear up under it."

Temptation is a test of man's free will; therefore, God can't take away his alternative to sin without destroying that same free will. So God does something just as effective for all who trust Him. He does something about the object of lust. He works outside of us at the very source of temptation.

That is best illustrated by a mother doing something about her child's temptation to steal cookies from a cookie jar. She can't whip the temptation out of him—so she simply puts the cookie jar "out of reach."

It is further illustrated by a father who moves his family away from a drug-infested neighborhood to keep his children from being seduced by narcotic users and pushers.

Parents have moved to a new continent to keep a son or daughter away from corrupting influences and friends.

These parents all acted in love, hoping their temporary intervention would allow time for their children to learn obedience from the heart. Although the time must come when children decide issues for themselves, a loving parent cannot stand idly by and allow an immature child to be overtaken by some evil influence. A concerned parent will either move the child away from the temptation or somehow put it out of his reach.

The Bible illustrates how God can put objects of temptation out of the reach of His children. For example, the children of Israel began to murmur against Moses for leading them out of Egypt. They wanted to go back to their old life-style. Freedom seemed too costly. So God arranged to open the Red Sea and allowed the Egyptian army to chase them across on dry land, then He closed up the sea—blocking any chance of return. God did that only in answer to the fervent prayers of Moses and other Israelites who wanted freedom.

Just as Jesus did, believers are to resist temptation with the Word of God. Most temptations can be defused by focusing the laser of truth on them. But there are other temptations that are so engrained, so furious and tenacious—they cannot be endured without supernatural intervention. The severest of temptations are often the result of a direct and personal attack by demonic powers.

Paul speaks of "fightings without, and fears within" (2

Corinthians 7:15). Satan actually declares war on certain converts who desert his army because they once best exemplified his power to possess. In his anger at losing such a "prize," he fights them from without by pounding on them with one severe temptation after another, to sift them as wheat. Jesus said to Peter, "Behold, Satan hath desired to have you, that he may sift you as wheat" (Luke 22:31). In other words, so shaken, you will hopefully break down.

Are you a believer who is being pounded by a recurring temptation that seems beyond your strength to resist? Is it a habit you can't control? Those involved with illicit secret lovers are especially overwhelmed by crushing temptations. So often, they yield and are soon swallowed up in remorse, guilt, and feelings of helplessness. If they are believers, they don't doubt that Christ has freed them from all obligations to obey the lust of their flesh. And, in many areas of their lives, they have seen progress and victory. Yet, there remains one besetting sin—one overpowering temptation to give in to a certain lust.

Thank God, there is a way of escape! God is a "miraculous intervener." It took a storm and a whale and a lot of supernatural intervention to get Jonah out of trouble. God has been known to turn water "bitter" and to cause manna to "stink," in an effort to make obedience less difficult.

God, in answer to fervent prayer, can make your object of lust become an abominable stench to you, and He can make yielding to sin become so bitter, you will hesitate to ever give in again. He may detour you; He may remove people from your life; He may cause the object of your lust to turn against you; He may throw up all kinds of roadblocks; He may throw up a "Job wall" of protection; He may simply draw you irresistibly into the secret closet of prayer; He may send someone to warn or correct you—but in one supernatural way or another, God will answer prayer and intervene, making it possible for believers to overcome their most violent temptations.

Those who, deep inside, don't want to give up their lust and who secretly hope to keep on indulging it can never receive this miraculous intervention when being tempted. God moves in to make a way of escape only when the heart is fully committed to a life of separation and purity.

If there is not such a commitment, it won't work. God is not obligated to intervene when someone really doesn't want deliverance.

Flirters with secret sin are left to fight temptation with their own strength. Then when they yield to sin, they blame God for not "pulling them out." They say, "I waited for God, but He just let me go ahead and do it."

But the believer who honestly wants to be free from sin's bondage can be assured his loving Father sees his struggle and will use all the power of Heaven to assist him.

When severely tempted, ask God for His supernatural intervention, and ask in faith, believing He will do it.

God has promised to "deliver us from all evil." Here is proof of God's help in time of temptation:

Ye that love the Lord, hate evil: he preserveth the souls of his saints; he delivereth them out of the hand of the wicked.

Psalms 97:10

We have escaped with our lives as a bird from a hunter's snare. The snare is broken and we are free!

Psalms 124:7 TLB

My eyes are ever looking to the Lord for help, for he alone can rescue me.

Psalms 25:15 TLB

So shall they fear the name of the Lord from the west, and his glory from the rising sun. When the enemy shall come in like a flood, the Spirit of the Lord shall lift up a standard against him.

Isaiah 59:19

I need no longer fear slipping or falling. He will keep me, love me, and bring me to glory by His power.

And he is able to keep you from slipping and falling away, and to bring you, sinless and perfect, into his glorious presence with mighty shouts of everlasting joy.

Jude 24 TLB

7

How to End Your Struggle

A leader of the Gay Coalition in San Francisco wrote the following about this author: "Mr. Wilkerson is a fanatic who strangely concerns himself with the private and personal sexual preferences of others. He is a reactionary who is narrow-minded, and the most laughable thing is that he has the ludicrous notion that homosexuals want to become straight because they have another 'evil' self inside them, making them perform unholy acts. I am a very happy homosexual with no guilt feelings or 'evil' influences consuming me from inside. People with guilt are just not stable people to start with— they would have problems whether they were gay or straight. Only total weaklings talk of so-called 'healing.' "

I have nothing but pity for the sinners who no longer

admit to an inner struggle with evil. They no longer struggle because they have surrendered to their evil passions. The Bible refers to such people as being "dead in trespasses and sins." Paul said of them:

> They live in a world of shadows, and are cut off from the life of God through their deliberate ignorance of mind and sheer hardness of heart. They have lost all decent feelings and abandoned themselves to sensuality, practising any form of impurity which lust can suggest.
>
> Ephesians 4:17–19 PHILLIPS

The person God is interested in is the one who battles heroically against his evil shadow self and who feels sorrow and guilt after giving in to temptation. The struggle itself is proof enough that the heart is still crying out to God for help. There is hope for one who is still experiencing an inner battle. The struggle against sin in the life of an honest person is evidence that he or she refuses to give in to its power. The difference between a sinner and a Christian is how one views sin. The Christian hates his sin; the sinner excuses and justifies it.

God's supernatural help is promised to those who thrash about in the deep, dark womb of evil, struggling to be free. And the surest sign that new life is springing up in the sinner is the urgency to cry out. All newborn children cry as soon as they come to life. Those who cry are really on the verge of a new life.

The first step toward ending your inner struggle is to learn how to cry. Are you tired of all the emptiness, loneliness, the despair and restlessness? Then let the tears flow unashamedly. Cry out all the pent-up desperation. Humble yourself and let the hurts and grief caused by sin pour out of your innermost being. The Bible urges you to cry out to God in your hour of distress. The cry of desperation is the key to all freedom from sin.

Here is Bible proof:

In my distress I called upon the Lord, and cried unto my God: he heard my voice out of his temple, and my cry came before him, even into his ears.

Psalms 18:6

This poor man cried and the Lord heard him, and delivered him out of all his troubles.

Psalms 34:6

He . . . heard my cry. . . . He brought me up also out of a horrible pit, out of the miry clay, and set my feet upon a rock, and established my goings.

Psalms 40:1, 2

"Your cry came to me at a favorable time, when the doors of welcome are wide open. . . ." Right now God is ready to welcome you. Today he is ready to save you.

2 Corinthians 6:2 TLB

The second step is to cultivate a sorrow for your sins and confess them to Christ. When you cry out to God, He draws near to you with His awesome holiness and love. You will know, without a doubt, when God and you are closing the gap between you. His holy presence growing stronger in your life will produce a grief and sorrow for all the sins, selfishness, and pride you have been guilty of. The closer you get to God, the more you feel the pain and guilt for past sins. But that guilt and sorrow is a wonderful thing; don't try to run from it. Let it become even more intense, because that is the only path to true repentance and forgiveness. The Bible says:

> Godly sorrow brings repentance that leads to salvation and leaves no regret, but worldly sorrow brings death. See what this godly sorrow has produced in you . . . what eagerness to clear yourselves . . . alarm. . . .
>
> 2 Corinthians 7:10, 11 NIV

A heart that is truly sorry wants to be forgiven. Paul said, "You sorrowed to repentance" (2 Corinthians 7:9). In other words, "You were sorry enough to confess and forsake your sins." You will discover a peace you never thought possible the moment you lay down your sins and accept forgiveness and mercy.

> He that covereth his sins shall not prosper: but whoso confesseth and forsaketh them shall have mercy.
>
> Proverbs 28:13

> Repent and be converted that your sins may be blotted out.
>
> Acts 3:19

Repentance is more than just saying, "God, I'm sorry! I feel pretty bad about all the evil things I've done."

That is sorrow, but not repentance. When God says repent of your sins, He really means: Turn your back on them. Learn to hate the things you once loved, and learn to love the things you once hated. That is a complete turnaround, a willingness to forsake old friends and habits for a new life in Christ. He is not trying to change you just so you can conform to the social values of others, but rather that you may experience the total joy and indescribable freedom known only to those who surrender to Christ. Self-conquest is possible only through surrender and devotion to Christ. We are to "yield ourselves" to Him.

> None of you can be my disciple unless he forsakes everything he has and follows me.
>
> Luke 14:33

Next, accept your forgiveness by faith and shut your ears to all the roaring lies of Satan. Study the following Scriptures; believe they are meant for you; and do what God asks. Here is the truth that can set you free and help you to forever end your struggle.

> If we confess our sins, he is faithful and just to forgive us of our sins, and to cleanse us from all unrighteousness.
>
> 1 John 1:9

> Whosoever shall confess that Jesus is the Son of God, God dwelleth in him, and he in God.
>
> 1 John 4:15

> If you confess that Jesus is Lord and believe that God raised him from death, you will be saved. For it is by our faith that we are put right with God; it is by our confession that we are saved. The scripture says, "Whoever

believes in him will not be disappointed." This includes
everyone. . . . "Everyone who calls out to the Lord for
help will be saved."

Romans 10:9–13 TEV

Believe on the Lord Jesus Christ and thou shalt be saved.

Acts 16:31

Therefore, if anyone is in Christ, he is a new creation; the
old has gone, the new has come.

2 Corinthians 5:17 NIV

Now, pray the following simple prayer and expect
God to hear it and forgive and cleanse you from all your
sins.

I here and now confess with my mouth that Jesus Christ is
Lord—that He is the very Son of God. I repent and admit
I am a sinner. I confess to Him all my sins. I am sorry. I
believe in Him with all my heart. By faith, I accept forgiveness for all my sins, and do now acknowledge that I
am a new person, born into the family of God. By faith I
am reborn, and this is the first day of my new life serving
Christ as a free person.

One final word: Don't ever again be afraid of any
evil presence in your life. Enter into the rest God has
promised you—and from this day forward, *keep your
momentum.*

The most important thing I can say to a believer who
is sincerely battling a secret sin is: Keep your momentum! No one has ever drowned when swimming up-
stream toward Christ. No one is left bleeding by the
wayside if he is wounded in his struggle to be free.

When you fall or when you are face to face with an addiction that won't let go, God draws a line right where you are. He says, "Get up; confess; and keep moving on. Don't cross back over the line. Don't go back to slavery. Keep coming to Me. You have been emancipated, so keep your momentum toward your freedom, by faith."

The most important move you ever make, as a believer, is the move you make right after you fall. Satan whispers, "You are rotten to the core, sensuous, childish, immature. You will never be holy; you will never be anything in God. So quit! Give up. It's useless to try. Go back! God is too high and holy; it's too complicated and difficult; you'll never figure it out. It's all over!"

Lies—all lies! So you sinned after you confessed and believed? So you thought you had freedom and lost it? So you think people will call you a phoney? So you sinned with your eyes wide open—knowing better— with the Holy Spirit screaming in your ears? So you never thought you could do such a vile thing again? So what? Is there godly sorrow in you now? Are you determined to get up and move on? Are you humbled, shamed, and repentant? Your fall is not fatal. Once again, confess and accept God's forgiveness and regain your momentum! You are still His child. You are not a slave to sin. His loving-kindness is greater than all your sins. Look up, rejoice, and take heart!

Stop your everlasting introspection. You won't find victory, probing around the garbage dump of your evil nature. That would be like a losing general's crossing the enemy lines to consult with his foe, asking, "Can you please tell me what I'm doing wrong? I want to defeat you, but I can't seem to make headway. What am I doing wrong?"

Right direction doesn't come by understanding the wrong. It comes only by understanding and claiming the bountiful promises of God in Christ Jesus. So quit looking inward; look up to Him who loves you at all times. Stop trying to figure yourself out, and rejoice in His restoring, healing love.

> For God is at work within you, helping you want to obey him, and then helping you do what he wants.
>
> Philippians 2:13 TLB

> There still exists therefore, a full and complete rest for the people of God. And he who experiences his rest [has quit the struggle] is resting from his own work. . . . Let us then be eager to know this rest for ourselves, and . . . beware that no one misses it through falling into unbelief. . . .
>
> Hebrews 4:9–11 PHILLIPS

For further information
or additional copies, contact

David Wilkerson
Garden Valley Publishers
P.O. Box 951
Lindale, Texas 75771

Keep the Hot Line Hot

Every Christian has a hot line direct to the Father. Whether our Christian walk leaps briskly forward or grinds to a halt depends on whether we make proper use of the privilege of prayer. Some of the foremost Christian writers of our day specifically address themselves to this vital concern. Their experience and insight are yours for the reading.

These best-selling authors have guided millions to abundant and self-fulfilling Christian living!